All is Quiet:
Man and His Fate

All is Quiet: Man and His Fate

By
A.H.G.

E-BookTime, LLC
Montgomery, Alabama

All is Quiet: Man and His Fate

Library of Congress Control Number: 2008906045

ISBN: 978-1-59824-864-7

First Edition
Published July 2008
E-BookTime, LLC
6598 Pumpkin Road
Montgomery, AL 36108
www.e-booktime.com

For then there will be a great tribulation, such as has not occurred since the beginning of the world until now, nor ever will.

Matthew 24:21

Preface

This book was written in accordance with the events that are taking place right now and which will take place in the near future throughout the world and within its society that brings us ever closer to the destruction of mankind. This is not written to act as a guide or for one to follow, but as a means to open up the readers mind as to what is possibly going to take place and that we as people should be prepared for.

I have strived to make this book as simple as possible to the reader without writing hundreds of pages. These writings are here for the reader to be warned of the global events that may soon take place when we least expect it. And that these warnings are going unnoticed to many within the human race as we wake each day. I have for the lack of better words- cut right to the chase in terms of the coming fate that so readily awaits man and the world he currently lives in if he does not make a great effort to change his ways soon. This book was designed to open up the reader to the truth about today's modern society in its entire works.

We live in very excited times right now in this day and age with all the new and increasing development of technology and research, escalating wars, and domestic violence within each nation of the world. I am here with the intent to try and explain to you the direction that of which mankind is so blindly treading the path to and that it should not be so blindly ignored.

By choosing to read these writings you have taken the initiative to open a new sight or view in terms of what all of humanity will possibly experience in the coming future.

Dear Reader,

I am no messenger nor am I a prophet. I am not here to write a 300 page book to try and tell you how to live and what to believe or not to believe. I am not here to tell you where to put your faith and what religion to join or cult for that matter. But what I can tell you is that I believe man's fate grows closer as each day passes by and that many people are oblivious to these signs and warnings that were put here for us. Or they just don't want to think about them. I am not telling you that after reading this book to go and stand on a street corner with a huge sign around your body and waving a bible in your hand shouting to the world that the end is here. Nor am I trying to strike fear into you by telling you to hide out in your house and bolt your doors and windows. **That is the media's job to do that.** As far as I am concerned you can toss away this book and never have to look at it again. Of course the decision is yours to go on reading these words and only yours by choice.

I believe there to be many sources that give credible evidence that mankind may meet his fate sooner than we all think.

There have been numerous books written on what I am here to tell you of and that is why my goal is to make this as basic as possible and to try and make you understand what could *possibly* happen in the near future and that every human being should be very alert and prepared for what may lay ahead.

With war and famine, strife, and increasing disasters, exploding populations, rising gas and oil prices, cost of food, domestic violence, terrorism, and immorality all growing at an increasing rate everyday, all this that stirs in the pot of evil is soon to boil over within this world and society we currently inhabit and may scorch many leaving a scar upon the flesh of man. Many would say that yes, this just may as well be the end of the world. The end of mankind and all that he created will soon come to a halt and cease to exist no more. But what if the world did not end as most say it would. What would happen then?

Dear reader, do not take these writings you are about to read too lightly. Take heed and observe the world events that are taking place right now before your very eyes and that are soon to take place in the coming future.

Contents

"I will punish the world for its evil,
and the wicked for their iniquity ...
I will halt the arrogance of the proud."

Isaiah 13:11

Predicting The End Times

For many years throughout history of mankind the prediction of the end of humanity was sought after by many religious groups and cults that were founded on this very source. Unfortunately many groups, mainly cults have put them-selves in bad situations by following these so called leaders that have claimed to know when the end of the world was. Many have paid the consequences with even their lives because they chose to blindly follow a false prophet. By far none of these groups have been proven right.

But we must not search for clues and sources from just these modern days, but to go back in time to the ancient civilizations that once flourished throughout the world. There are numerous ancient cultures that were believed to know of certain events throughout time through prediction by looking towards the heavens (the night sky) for their answers. And by learning and gaining a great deal of knowledge about the earth and its universe they were able to predict with complete accuracy planetary events and activities that were to take place. One such culture we are all most familiar with is the ancient Mayan culture. The Mayans have been well known for their accurate calendar of events and time and were also geniuses when it came to mathematics. The reason why I along with everyone else chose this certain culture is the fact that everyone is most familiar with their astonishing prediction concerning the end of civilization. One being that we all have heard of is the halt of human existence on the year 2012. It would be greatly argued by many of today exactly what this calendar event *truly* means. Does it mean the end of mankind? Or does it mean a new beginning for mankind? I am not to go too much into detail regarding the ancient Mayan culture. That is for the reader to do on their own time. Another is the planetary alignment or celestial alignment that is going to take place very soon. Again, predicted by not only the Mayans, but other credible sources as well.

Another source I believe to be *somewhat* credible is a man whom we are all familiar with by the name of Nostradamus. Many have written numerous books on him and many documentaries have been broadcasted throughout the world regarding his predictions. Though many believe that the Nostradamus predictions are very vague in description, I believe that one may find his predictions quite fascinating and therefore should be a source to compare with others in order to make sense of what may possibly lie ahead for mankind and that his predictions should not be taken too lightly. **(We have just recently discovered the illustrations that were hidden away for quite some time now that the reader should be aware of concerning Nostradamus' predictions and that some would say that a picture is worth a thousand words.** *I believe it was just recently discovered for a reason to give warning for mankind).* Of course many would argue and say that Nostradamus was a man of little meaning and that his predictions meant nothing and are of little value to consider the fate of mankind. This of course is up to the reader to go out on their own and research Nostradamus and his teachings. When dealing with predictions from such men as Nostradamus, we must keep a complete open mind. The reason being is soon to be explained in the following writings of this book. After all, how many people of this modern day and age can have visions such as Nostradamus and be willing to make them public?

Another among the credible sources I believe to be of great importance and value is that of the bible. Though written for the sole purpose of benevolence towards our fellow human beings and a means of how man should live his life, it gives many warnings in *great* detail on what will happen to this world and man. From the Book of Daniel to the Book of Revelations being the last chapter of the bible, many have sought and turned to these readings to seek answers for the end times. By far the bible has proven to be one the most invaluable tools out there in regards of seeking information concerning man's fate. It should also be noted that it is still the number one leading book to be sold on the market today. The reader will also notice quite a few quotes that I have put into this book that are taken from the bible. The reason being as I have stated before, the bible is by far the most credible tool there is out there right now. (*A person does not have to be religious to turn to the bible for information regarding the end times*).

An even more interesting source leading to man's fate can be that of the bible codes that were just recently discovered by man using our great piece of technology called the computer to decipher meanings in the Jewish text, the Torah. As introduced on television which I am sure we are familiar with are the codes being found within the texts of the bible discussing the past events that had already taken place *and* the future events that are to *supposedly* soon take place. Now here again we find that the codes of the bible poses as a controversial and delicate subject for anyone. One I believe that should also not be taken too lightly by man. We will find out more on why the bible codes also play an important role when it comes to credible sources in the later writings. **(We must ask ourselves why suddenly in these perilous times we live in; the bible codes were just discovered. By such recent discoveries, what is it that man is trying to be told)?**

There are a few other credible sources that the reader must be aware of and that is one being the ever increasing wars that are taking place right now in this day and age. It is not just ground combat anymore with man or machine. Now it is the fact that one button can be pushed from the comfort of a chair to launch a major man-made catastrophic event bringing utter annihilation to mankind around the globe. With the advantages of being able to detonate in the air or on the ground with thousands of degrees behind its destructive force it can wipe out millions of people with its raw power. Yes, it is as we all know to be the nuclear weapon of the modern ages. With many countries now seeing that they too can have a nuclear device the threat of nuclear destruction is at its all time highs right now. This is just a small source we can depend on to figure out why man's fate is closely at hand.

One other credible source I would also like for the reader to be aware of is the doomsday clock. The doomsday clock is said to be a symbol of the minutes away mankind is to self destruction. Maintained since the year 1947 by the Board of Directors of the Bulletin of the Atomic Scientists at the University of Chicago it uses the hands of a clock to show how many minutes away man is to midnight from a complete all out nuclear war from around the globe. As the reader may discover after observing the clock, it will show five minutes away from midnight. Updated periodically we will see it move closer to the stroke of midnight. This credible source will soon play its role in the preceding writings that will lead us to believe that a major change may soon *possibly* unfold before our eyes.

*"Because lawlessness is increased,
most people's love will grow cold"*

Matthew 24:12

The Evil Within Mankind

What is evil? Or what is considered to be evil? One may find that evil is anything that of course opposes good. It will also depend on the type of person that may view what they think is evil. What may be evil to one person may not be considered evil to another, but what is to be noted in these next writings is the fact that evil can come in many forms and that who ever possess this quality will go about using it to harm the good of his own species and other species as well...

As the reader already may have noticed the quote that was mentioned on the previous page indicates that each day that is given to man brings new births of hatred and anger that cultivate within the minds of people in the society of today.

Since the beginning of man evil has always tried to worm its way into the thoughts and the very soul of the individual. <u>I must note to the reader that in these next writings it may seem like I am getting into the psychological aspect of evil within the minds of many.</u> <u>That is because one must understand what evil can bring to man's actions and what major role it plays in the fate of all who inhabit this earth and the destruction it will bring to many by all who as so much abide by its existence.</u> From the mind of the individual out on the streets to the very heart of terrorism from around the globe, evil plays an important part in the fate of mankind. Evil is all the same when it comes to its form in general. Depending on the mind of the individual it currently feeds upon directs to what actions they will take and how one would put evil to use against another to do harm. Evil is everywhere we look. We can find it on such tools as the television and radio. We will even find it when we step out of our houses to go to the market or wherever our destination may be. It is in our schools, businesses, and even in some of our churches. When we go to turn on the news in the morning after waking up or at the end of the day when we come home from work all we hear is how someone was shot that day or stabbed, raped or kidnapped, severely beaten, and terrorized in different ways. We hear of wars, famine, and corruption in not only where we live, but from all around the world. The reader must note to themselves that they too can see with their eyes that man's love *does* grow colder as each day comes to pass. Whenever one drives to work they can view it out on the streets. With so much people out on the roads it has increased rage in the individual by an astronomical percentage and can breed new feelings such as hate and anger and large amounts of impatience or increase those feelings much greater than they already are. Now nobody is perfect as we may already know it, but what I am trying to point out to the reader is that we can see that all I mentioned in the above will grow at an increasing rate day by day. And the more it does, the more we will hear about it. The more the population increases, the more the above increases in the individual and the more others are affected by it. A small and perfect example that I will speak of when it comes to evil out on the streets is that of the individual driver that is in a hurry to get where they need or want to be. A classic example, the person behind you can be in a hurry and purposely speed up to where they are inches away from coming in contact with your vehicle. If you were to have to make an immediate stop they would have obviously hit you from behind due to their foolishness. Now the reader should imagine what if the person who was hit was a female with child or had a small child in the vehicle with them? Or what if they were to possess a weapon of some sort and use it against the other? This is the term we use as road rage. Now the person who is following closely behind you may not be in a hurry, but may deliberately be closing in on your vehicle for the sole purpose of getting you to move out of their way. Now what the reader must be extremely aware of is the fact that this person who is following closely behind them on purpose possesses the possibility of a certain degree of hate and anger or perhaps impatience within them. This of course would most likely lead to verbal violence and then to threaten with physical violence if there was to be an accident. Of course from the accident the person from behind would be blinded by their evil feelings towards the other even though they were at fault. Now a small percentage of other people would not allow such feelings of aggression to come into play during a scenario as this. But what I am to point out is the fact that the greater percentage of people in this society would allow these feelings to foolishly blind them for whatever reason it may be, whether they are having a bad day or other types of feelings therefore bringing harm to another or possibly even bringing harm to their own being. Another great example would be a person who would purposely or by accident cut another driver off. What would most people do in this case if they were cut off suddenly? They would purposely speed up right on the other persons vehicle acting with such aggression and hostility towards them therefore creating more of a problem for them that can result in a much more violent act. Instead of slowing down and staying a good deal of distance behind the person that cut right in front of them, one would most likely choose to allow a malevolent feeling overcome them and cloud their rational thoughts and judgment.

The reader can clearly view these acts being committed all the time by observing the many types of drivers there are out on the streets of today's society and be able to see how hostility towards their fellow man comes into play and what it may possibly lead to. *What these individual's do not realize is that each time they conjure up a feeling of bad nature towards another they are allowing the feelings of hatred or anger to grow stronger and stronger from within their mind and soul each time they bring it forth, therefore feeding it constantly and with the possibility of them being led to commit a foolish act of evil towards another if it grows out of hand allowing these hateful feelings to eat them up from within.* It is a perfect example of the love that grows cold as each day passes within many of today's society. If someone was to be struck by a driver of these days the driver would most likely not stop to help the injured, but would speed away making it as we know it to be a hit and run scenario. Sometimes we are minding our own business in society and we come across an individual who possesses much hatred and anger within themselves for whatever reason it may be. If we were to do something that this individual does not like even though it was on accident or even if it posed as no serious threat such as a glance or a non threatening comment in their direction this individual would most likely commit a harsh action against the innocent whether it be verbal *or* in today's society most likely lead to physical violence and have the high possibility of leading to a life taken. Instead of not taking a more civilized action to a scenario such as this, the individual would allow the evil within them to take over their thoughts clouding their judgment and do much harm to the other. **This is what grows in man each day**.

Sadly enough we can hear of this evil in our schools. As the years progress we can hear of more and more students being terrorized by an individual or individuals on the school campuses. What I find to be most amazing and disturbing is the fact that even now elementary schools where children are sent to learn and play are being targeted by this form of evil. One can hear of a small child severely beating another child to almost near death or even taking weapons to school with the intent of committing an evil act such as taking ones life for no reason at all. Of course we should note that it *does* in fact come down to the parents which are in charge of the up bringing of the child. We can also note that sadly without the counseling of the small child in the proper manner may most likely lead to the cultivation of anger and hatred within the child throughout their years of maturing and that it may someday lead to evil acts being committed by this individual in their adulthood life.

Another form of evil one must come to realize is the fate of the churches that have corruption from within. As I am sure the reader is familiar with is that of the Catholic Church and its devastating hidden immoral practices from these so called men

21

of God by the name of *priests* that was just recently discovered and made public. Since then the Catholic Church has faced many hardships from not only the mind of large organizations but to the very mind of the single individual of today. This is just another form of evil that goes on in today's world. As sad as it may seem the Catholic Church is now left with a permanent scar marked upon them.

I am to explain in these next writings there is a very large scale that has grown in the sense of evil and will continue to grow at an increasing rate and pose as a serious threat too many throughout the years to come. We all know it as terrorism which is the form of a group of people by means of using massive radical movements in order to get their message across by the use of utter violence. Throughout history there has been terrorism by different groups of religions and ethnicity for many different causes. I am to speak of terrorism mainly in the Middle East where it has been going on there for centuries and sadly will continue to go on through the years to come. And the fact that right now certain countries are dealing with mainly the terrorists from the Middle East. The main fight one will notice today with terrorism would be about race and religion. We can hear today that it is said to them to destroy all those who are not like them and that it has even been pointed out by many that their god tells them to use the means of violence to get their message across. From the suicide bombings to the shootings of small children it is disgusting to know and hear that this is what they believe in and will find paradise for such evil acts in the end. With the ever increasing nuclear weapons that play its role in massive destruction it is now a major concern among many regarding terrorists. Many people fear of a nuclear weapon finding its way into the hands of today's modern terrorist.

Now that a spark has been ignited and the flames have spread through the entire world in this form, terrorism is now our number one concern when it comes to the evils that stir in the mind of man. I am to point out another thought that the reader must keep in mind and that is when evil is cultivating within man, one must be aware of the severe consequences it can bring upon many that it will affect. Whether it be a common man in the street which would possess a weapon that would threaten those that are around him to one who is given a certain position of power and a role to play for a whole nation of people it can be a danger for that of mankind. I will give a slight example: take the common man of low rank that walks amongst us in society who is capable of committing such evil acts of aggression against another by using any means of violence with any weapon of such. We can see that this person with their evil act can affect a small amount of others from his wrong doings. Now let's take a man of high rank in society that is given the position and power by certain parties to use his acts that would affect the way people live and think. What if this man of high rank was to possess a certain quality of evil within him? Given his status in society an act of evil that he would use against others would not only be a severe blow to a person or small group of people, but would be detrimental for a whole nation and perhaps reach out even further beyond that. There is another fact that needs to be noted here in regards of evil within our society and that is corruption from within our authorities who are suppose to protect and serve the citizens of communities. One can find that they share their part when it comes to evil acts. Now the question is, "who is going to police the police?"

We can realize that our children of today cannot go and play outside without the thought of them being kidnapped or harmed from another human being in any way.

What can be found most shocking in today's society is the thought that violence is so common these days that we can observe television programs showing nothing but hours of back to back episodes of violent ruthless acts of evil being committed and caught on camera. And many allow their small children to witness these ridiculous television programs.

Of course I must point out that there are still many other acts of evil that flourish throughout the world right now, but as a reminder to the reader I am here again trying to stay with the basics that one can understand and grasp without a great deal of trouble understanding it.

All Eyes Have Opened

*T*he day of a world super power is now at its beginning stages and all are aware that anything goes.

Yes, it is truly another arms race of the modern day for man. With many countries from around the world now seeing that they too can have a part to play in a world power many have congregated together and have started the rebuilding and reuniting of a new nation and many will be sure to come. With nation now turning against nation, one could not help but to imagine what may possibly lay ahead for the entire world to witness. Many nations now see that others can no longer seem to maintain their status in some aspects of being the strongest and now have seemed to have discovered their weaknesses. It does not take much research for the reader to do in order to find out that nations are slowly turning against each other. All one has to do is turn to the headlines on television to realize the direction we are all taking.

Wars in general have been made throughout time since man has first perceived evil in his thoughts and learned to brandish weapons for the sole purpose of destruction against another. From the streets within our society to the broader wars that are fought overseas, wars can be caused by anybody about anything. Of course we are familiar with all the wars that we studied while we were attending elementary school and through our way into college. One must observe that with the weakening structures of some nations and growing stability of others that it now poses as what we all know it to be the classic saying "survival of the fittest." The reader will notice that the countries that were thought to be of weak nature in military and governance have now made the advancements to a slightly higher level of status on the scale of the world; if not - a greater advancement.

One mistake that can be realized is that of the under-estimation by many nations of their enemies or who would be classified as an enemy. We should note a very important point of view here, and that is one should never underestimate a person or country for any matter. Just because we hear of a certain country that may have disastrous issues in the sense of corruption within their government regarding shortages of food or a lack of sophisticated technology and so forth does not mean that one should shun them aside and pay no attention to them. This of course can lead to a serious threat on ones behalf in future events.

In these next writings I am to discuss in minute detail on why certain countries have fallen and others have flourished. Part of the reason has to do with not getting involved in war and meddling in the business of other countries unless otherwise asked too. It is to be pointed out that it does take a strong and bold country to come to the aid of others when in need- and I say, **when in need.** Not just to go and conquer for the sole purpose of a resource that one might need or because there is a personal vengeful act that is going to be committed. Countries have felt the hardship of getting involved in a conflict with another by means of aggression and therefore have put them in a bad situation that has affected their stability in most aspects. Then there are those countries that choose to stay neutral throughout many years therefore giving them the ability to increase their strength in terms of the economic value, military strength, research and development and many other great achievements. Of course this will lead one to a better position in the world than they currently already maintain. It is common sense I am speaking of here; I will let the reader try and figure it out for themselves. Now we come to the country that possesses a weak quality in overall. This is because of their leaders. **A quick note:** depending on what type of leader a country has and the quality they possess will determine the country's overall stability in every category. A poor leader leading a poor country will meet its poor fate. A perfect example: I am to speak of a certain country in the Middle East that we are all familiar with that once held a leader of poor quality that met his own poor fate in the end. This leader was selfish in thought and used funds that the country had to build extremely elaborate mansions and estates just for the sole purpose of greed and glamour. Instead of using the funds in a much wiser sense such as the building of a new economy and the survival of his people and the overall strengthening of his country, he chose to take the path of evil and used the resources for such evil acts.

In all the examples I have stated in the above comes down to one thing and that is throughout the years to come new leaders will be born. When those new leaders are born come new ways of thinking and create new disagreements therefore having the possibility of one turning against the other and creating wars against each other. We all must be aware that wars will increase through the years to come and that we will start to see leaders disagreeing with each other and starting to slowly break away from the chain of trust leading us closer and closer into the ever increasing fate that awaits mankind. Even now as this is being read there are rumors of wars and preparations being made by certain countries steadily readying to go into a full launched assault with others on a massive scale with the possibility of leading ourselves into the next world war; this time perhaps even more devastating than the last.

Even The Strongest Of Nations Have Fallen

As it was with ancient Rome, it can be and will be for the Rome of modern cities of today. We are all familiar with the rise and fall of the Roman Empire in ancient times. Let us reflect on what has brought this mighty nation down to its knees. With all the wealth and power a certain country or nation can possess does not mean it will remain so forever. Due to its constant replacement of leaders to lead these mighty countries it brings new thought and attitudes towards others and has led to collapse from within. It is the good leader that helps the country or people to prosper and maintain their status among the strong. A perfect example is the ruler ship of Gaius Octavian or as we are more familiar with Augustus Caesar. Nephew to Julius Caesar he was treated as a son to him and therefore taken under his wing to teach him on how to rule with greatness and gain the respect and loyalty of the roman people despite the civil confrontations going on between the Romans which were under leadership by Mark Antony. With this in mind he had achieved many great goals. Of course Rome before his time made many great accomplishments, but it was the fact that he brought it together in times of peril. **(Who will bring *our* Rome together in these times of peril?)**

But what of the leaders that came to take his place after his departure from this earth? We can learn that Rome was given leaders that thought nothing of them and tossed aside its people. We can also note that during this time of inane actions by these new leaders that it played a major role on the whole nation with such effects as the food shortages, increasing crime waves, increasing corruption from within the senate, and economic upheaval leading to the destruction from within the country. Augustus took the funds that were given to him and used it to benefit the nation and its people leading to a greater unity between the two.

But now what of the modern civilizations and how are they related to ancient history? The saying history repeats itself can be very true for anything that man encounters today. It goes for the nations of today in terms of leadership and value of each nation. Even to this very day and in future date as well it will depend on the greatness of leadership and the use of political power that is given to man in order to rule over one. What we learnt of throughout history can *and* should solely be implemented in today's increasing struggle for stronger nations and a more prosperous economy. another great example is that of Aristotle in his writings to the Great Alexander of Macedon as he went forth to conquer and lead the people of the nations, that if a leader set in his land evil customs and over pass the way of truth he will set no great laws and ways of living to help the people and therefore will win for himself the fame of evil. This simply means mistrust in the hearts and minds of the people in regards of their great leader that rules over them and will start the fall and tribulation of a nation.

All that has been given to the reader in these paragraphs is now occurring at this very moment with not only small countries, but large and powerful ones as well. If there is to be no change in political power with certain leaders than there is to be no change in the trouble that awaits the nations and its people. One can observe that history will always repeat itself no matter what the circumstances. As disturbing as it may sound, all it can take is one man to bring his fellow species to experience hardships and possibly experience major destruction.

The Boundaries Of Technology

With the ever increasing technology and research man is currently embarking on brings new meaning to what strategic role many will play in the global battlefront of today. I must also point out to the reader to be aware of the increasing knowledge man has gained and that it will continue to grow at a most incredible rate like never before, thanks to our new discoveries that are being made. Whether you choose to believe this or not this will also play a significant role in the fate of man. One can even hear of a very exciting race that a few countries are taking part in and that is the race to the planet of Mars.

From the very first computer to the small device we all carry around called the cellular phone man has truly made quite a dent in the area of technology. But what if we were to take it up to the next step? To further our study's beyond that of natural creation and existence and that of the natural law?

In these next writings I will strive to explain the limits which are being breached right now in this modern day and age when it comes to knew discoveries and the direction which man is taking in terms of knowledge and technology. We can also use this topic to further our perception or observation in the coming of man's fate and what role technology will play. The reader must realize that we have only begun to scratch the surface of technology although it may seem impressive with what we may already have produced, there is still much to come in the years ahead in our technological advancements. One would realize that as with power so can technology be used for good or for bad. One of the most controversial subjects in regards to how far technology has been taken is that of cloning DNA from other organisms by means of reproducing the exact same structure in all its matter. One can find this to be of great importance in the role it plays when we come to the boundaries and limitations of research and development. Many will also argue that it would be seen as a means of playing God. Such groups and organizations have protested against this subject and have even been condemned by religious sects. There is also the controversial matter of couples even being able to now choose what type of child they would like to have before it is even born into this world. I **humorously state-** *what make and model one can choose from and with the certain options (character traits of the child).* But now our limitations have reached even a little further beyond with that in mind. For example, it is said that there is a certain program which was started by an organization that can enable the puberty of a child to come to a halt, or drastically slow the process down in order to ask the parents or individual whether they want to be a female or male. Yes, as far fetched as it may seem, it is being studied and implemented right now. One other major breakthrough that our scientists of today have achieved is that of the cloned beating heart. The procedure involved taking the existing cells from a deceased heart so that only the skeleton that it created the shape of was left. Though this is a small step that has just begun one could state that it does in fact benefit us a great deal. I will point out to the reader that what I have just discussed in the above are the main concerns society should take into consideration when it comes to our expanding research and development.

Rebirth Of The Beasts

One other topic that I would like to discuss here on the ability of cloning is the fact that scientists and geneticists are looking into cloning the unthinkable. And that is the man made reproduction of the once existing dinosaurs. What was once thought to only be movie material for the entertainment of an audience is now being done right now at this moment throughout laboratory's around the world. One might be familiar with the movie Jurassic park where the dinosaurs were being cloned for the purpose of an amusement park. Just recently it has been discovered by paleontologists that small tissue fibers have been found to still be somewhat active in fossilized bones that have been around for millions of years imbedded in the earth. We are now being able to extract the DNA from that source. We must realize that we are still quite a ways from ever cloning a dinosaur. Though the movie made it seem so simple, it would still pose as a much more difficult task for man to decipher in the laws of genetics.

But we must not forget that there was a reason that the dinosaurs became extinct. And that is because man and dinosaurs could not inhabit the earth at the same time.

To Live And To Live

One other curiosity that many people have often wondered about is immortality. It has been in the mind of man for many years on how one can never grow old or die. It has been among those questions that have plagued the very thoughts of humans. How can I live longer or stay younger? It has been studied that there are ways of staying healthier and maintaining an image of youth in many peoples of different ethnicity. We can see that in other countries people have known how to take care of their appearances and know ways to help maintain their feel of youth by means of certain extractions from plants and animals and by consuming certain types of food. Along with getting some exercise. With the increasing products that are out there in the market right now on anti aging and ways of looking younger, people have often wondered if there is ever going to be a product that can truly prevent one from decaying as they become older. At this moment scientists and researchers are trying to come up with ways in creating immortality.

There is a very important fact that should be pointed out here to the reader. Now what I am about to state may seem like I may be trying to force a religious belief upon one, but the truth of the matter is if it were intended for man to possess the trait of immortality then man would have eaten from the Tree of Life when the creator gave the Garden of Eden to Adam and Eve. Instead, man ate from the Tree of Knowledge therefore giving man today the knowledge that he possess. Now one would argue if man's knowledge grows at a tremendous rate then he would be able to figure out the formula for immortality. This of course would pose to be false for a couple reasons I am to explain. One reason would be that if man was to discover how to become truly immortal then all explanations and questions that people so dearly hold in their hearts would defeat the purpose of life and where we go when we are to leave this earth. The cycle of life would cease to exit no more. Another reason that would be of concern would be the population of the world. Of course there can be many other reasons as to why *true* immortality will most likely never be found or achieved amongst mankind. But as of right now for the time being many people will just rely on the anti aging products that are being produced right now and will only have the thought of age prevention in their mind when it comes to the subject of not being able to grow old. To most, true immortality is only a thing that can be observed in movies and science fiction.

Other amazing breakthroughs in technology I am eager to mention is the fact that recently it was shown and brought out to the public on the use of **Force Field technology.** We are now able to deflect any type of rocket propelled explosive or projectile within a few feet from impact on a target bringing the total percentage of damage down to about an amazing one percent that would be caused by an enemy. One other such piece of technology that greatly enhances military capabilities is that of the newly created ray gun. As seen in Science fiction movies and comic books we are now able to bring forth what would have seemed almost impossible at that time and something to only be of fantasy and be able to use it against an enemy or perhaps as was shown in a demonstration, a way to control large crowds or riots. Though we cannot actually see the ray or beam itself one could still feel the affect of the heat it generates from a great distance. The reader will also know there are other amazing creations made by man for the military that people needn't know about.

Space exploration has also greatly advanced in these past years. With unmanned space drones and satellites orbiting earth and also reaching deep into our solar system we are now permitted to observe the digital images that are rendered of never before seen footage outside our earth and also being able to catch numerous activities that are constantly taking place all the time. Man has been able to reap the benefits of learning how the certain planets are born. With this being said, it is able to greatly increase the knowledge of man at a tremendous rate therefore leaving us with a lot of answers on how the earth and other planets *might* have been created and also helping us to understand that there is a possibility of other life forms out there other than ours. We are also able to witness great events that take place within our sun that we are not able to view from earth. This too gives us a great amount of information as to why we experience certain solar phenomena and what effects it can have towards civilization. But of course this will be explained in later writings. We are just beginning to scratch the surface of deep space exploration in this modern age and yet there is still a great deal of discoveries we have yet to make.

I am to make a very important note to the reader and that is I believe there is very strong possibility that we as mankind may not be able to make it to the advancement of another planet in terms of starting a new civilization for mankind. The reason I believe this to be a problem is that man may not be meant to inherit another planet due to the fact that he cannot seem to control the planet that was greatly given to him and that the thought of corruption has been so wide spread throughout this world as it will for many years to come. There is the fact that war has always been in our blood and always will be. There is no point in bringing all that to a new planet. And one must not forget pollution also runs in mans nature. Why bring all these man made destructions to a virgin planet that has yet to be physically touched by the presence of man and his ways? We are already disgustedly destroying our planet in many ways, why another?

And what are we to make of wars? If mankind is destroying each other right now and always has been, why are we to wage war on another planet and bring upon the destruction of human civilization there? It only seems like common sense to figure all this out. But as I have stated before, with the increasing knowledge gained by man it *may* be possible and therefore people would be able to see the consequences that I have just discussed.

Of course there is a system that is called terraforming. And this simply means that all man made buildings and such would have to be indoors such as, farms, artificial lighting, man made oxygen and other materials if we would not be able to walk outside due to lack of oxygen or other potentially harmful substances that inhabits that certain atmosphere.

Another great source of new discoveries I would like to mention that is quite fascinating is that of new propulsion technology systems. Since the very first horse carriage to the modern jet turbine engines of today we are greatly working on improving new ways to propel our transportation to get to places a lot faster and safer. We are no longer just looking to use combustible engines anymore as a means of propulsion, but to now look to new ways of using propulsion on a whole different scale in the sense of vacuums that are created from high voltages of electricity in the air, one being from electrostatic fields. Another way of looking at it is electrogravatics in terms of anti gravity through the use of electricity. Many believe this to be the great technology by which extraterrestrial space crafts propel themselves at incredible velocities and are able to maneuver using centrifugal force by channeling that electricity to certain parts of their craft. Some might still argue that for now it is only theory. Of course I am not to go into great detail concerning this technology, but I only use this as a means of our ever growing thirst for sophisticated technological advancements. Our technology is also allowing us to find different fuel alternatives such as the use of corn oil other than gasoline or other combustible fuels.

Technology is also paving the way for advancement by the use of electric cars. Using the lithium ion batteries and hydrogen fuel cells as a way of propelling the vehicle we are able to travel to our destinations without having to worry about polluting the environment.

With the large surge in oil and gas prices that have greatly increased throughout the years at an alarming rate and the ever

waging wars that are to come it has caused these resources to become a very hot commodity. With gas prices at their all time highs one can only imagine the violence and hardships it will bring in the coming years. This is another good example of the many forms evil that has played in the lives of mankind and will play the part for quite awhile.

While it is to be noticed that there has always been raising and lowering of resources such as these it will only become worse each year as the wars grow stronger and the economies become weaker. This is part of the reason why scientists and researches are striving to find a better alternative fuel source and why we as man can also be grateful for the great technology we are being given. But will it be too late for a vast change in fuel technology?

Now in these next few paragraphs I am to explain the lighter side of our technology we currently have and put to great use in the medical field to help save ones life or better them in terms of health. One major discovery from medical science is that of the mechanical heart. In the event of a major heart difficulty that prevents a patient's heart from functioning properly we can turn to this little device and implant it within the person so that they may go on living a longer life. Another great use this generation possesses in the medical field are the use of CAT scans along with many other digital rendering devices that can detect many dysfunctions of the human body. I along with the reader would of course agree that we have certainly come a long way in the medical field of research and development for the caring of the sick and dying. The medical technology of today has given us a significant advantage over many areas of that field than twenty to thirty years ago and earlier.

There is a lot more technology out there that can come into great use by today's society such as robots, flying cars, and much more. To imagine what was and is seen in movies is now being literally brought to life in this day and age. Imagine the possibilities there will be when it comes to our future exploration in technology. What new benefits it will bring to mankind whether it is for personal use, medical, military and a lot more.

One could not help but to wonder where this civilization will be taken next.

From the life saving machines in our medical fields to the very machine conceived for the sole purpose of destruction on the battlefield man will always find ways of using his creations for good and evil.

"He answered and said to them,
. . . And there will be 'earthquakes in various (diverse) places,"

Matthew 24:8

"With Mars and Mercury and the Moon in conjunction,
Toward the south there will be extreme drought:
In the depths of Asia one will say the earth trembles,
Corinth, Ephesus then in a troubled state."

Nostradamus
Century III, Quatrain III

know as Global Warming. Many would say that it does not exist and others will say that it does. I am to point out to the reader that yes it does exist and that the threat is a very serious concern man must pay attention to. From Alaska the last frontier to Mount Kilimanjaro in Africa it does not take a scientist to realize that the earth is getting warmer each year. With all the snow melting in Alaska and around the world it does not only have an affect on the people that inhabit the regions, but the wildlife as well along with the total environment such as trees, plants, and insects. One can also observe Mount Kilimanjaro in Africa. Rising at a little over 15,000 ft. its peak once contained more snow covered areas all around its top in the past. But it is now sad that this once famous mountain is now losing its glaciers at an incredible 300 cubic meters a month due to high temperatures in climate change. Alaska among the many is experiencing these harsh changes. It is now said by the locals that each year more and more wildlife are forced to move towards the human civilization in search for food forcing literally animals and humans to live side by side from each other. I am to point out that Alaska is America's final frontier and that it is now slowly withering away. The same has to do with the giant glaciers that are floating in the oceans right now. All around the world they are melting into the water at an incredible rate therefore causing the sea levels to rise at an enormous rate each year. Where there were a great percentage of rainfalls around the globe in many regions they are now experiencing less. I find it quite disgusting to see and hear of certain parties on television and the radio make fun of people that try and help to warn humanity of the global warming event that is taking place. I along with many others have witnessed these people horribly mock those that are trying to get this serious message across to the world. And that is the fact we are endangering our planet and something needs to be done. This is what our society poses as. To mock those that are trying to help the good of mankind. Only to be stepped on and laughed at while being shunned away. And to think that these people that do this on television (as seen on a certain television show) make these foolish comments all for ratings and money. It is just in human nature to laugh and mock those that are trying to make a difference for the benefit of mankind.

Many civilizations around the world that have not already felt these effects of the increasing climate changes will do so more in the years to come. But one must ask the question, "Can we as humans stop this from happening?" I am to say that yes, we can. Can we fix the problem? We can. Though we cannot reverse it or if we could, it would take an extremely long time. But the damage has already been severely done and we must seek to preserve what little we will have left of it for our children and their children. We must realize that what problems we have caused will be left for the children of tomorrow to fix or deal with when it comes to the very health of our precious environment and the well being of human civilization.

Another interesting and yet disturbing thought is that from the earth's changing polarity that has been predicted by many. Even our modern day scientists have importantly stated that the planets will align every so many thousands of years and that it is poised to do so again very soon. Now we come too thought of what might happen to the earth's geographic regions due to this major event that is soon to take place. Will our weather be severely affected? Will there be great earthquakes caused as never before experienced by mankind that will bring major catastrophic blows to civilization? Know one knows what will truly happen when the time comes.

It has also been stated that the ocean's water levels will rise as I had previously mentioned. One may find that even right now they are rising due to the high rate of melting glaciers as the sun grows hotter each year. But what are the effects of the rising water levels? Will many regions be submerged under the water? Will deserts that see no ocean find itself a beach front? Will great cities from around the world that house millions of people become under water? Here again we must realize that nobody can know what will come due to this effect.

One is to note that the water levels are rising- this means that the tides will come in higher than they already are, therefore engulfing more land. Now I am to clearly state that when the waters become higher it poses a significant threat in terms of hurricanes and tsunamis. For example, if there were to be a great earthquake in magnitude in the ocean it would bring unthinkable colossal waves that have never before been heard of and truly swallow a whole city, or if not half of one. What I am trying to point out is that the reader must keep in mind the large quantities of water that have been given to the ocean by the melting of the glaciers. Just imagine the effects a tsunami would have if it were given twice or quadruple the force behind it in terms of hundreds of thousands of gallons of water when it was sweeping across the sea or over land. Yes, one can truly say that the ocean will overflow.

After a great misery, an even greater approach, the great motor of the cycles is renewed: Raining blood, milk, famine, iron and pestilence, (In the sky will be seen a fire, dragging a trail of sparks).

**Nostradamus
Century II, Quatrain 62**

We are all familiar with the extinction of the dinosaurs by the cataclysmic event that took place millions of years ago involving a massive meteorite that swept across the globe. This had caused a large scale impact that destroyed almost all life and had caused the sun to be blackened with major dust storms everywhere that covered the land. With this in effect there was no source of energy that was to be given to life and therefore caused the massive extinction of these great beasts that once ruled over the earth. Is there a great possibility this same event will unfold again?

It is also stated here that there is to be great disruptions from within our solar system that would come in contact with our earth. One is to speak of such great comets and asteroids that pose as a threat to the planet earth and everything that breathes within it. It is also stated in Revelations from the bible that tells of a coming of fire from the skies (space). As I had mentioned in previous writings that one does not have to be religious to turn the bible to find texts regarding comets and mankind. We can also use the source of the bible codes that do state a large asteroid that is said to be here by the year 2010. As the reader can clearly observe the quatrain that was given to us by Nostradamus is concerning a very large meteoroid otherwise known as an asteroid to come in contact with the human race.

Another threat that has become very real is that of our sun. It is known to all that without the energy of the sun life would not be able to survive as it currently does now. We look to the sun for many things such as energy for the growing of plants, solar panels that are now being used in many places to power devices, and many other uses. Other living creatures such as the shark for example, depend on warmer waters. It even has its uses for people when they want to get a tan at the beach or just go to the beaches when it comes to recreation.

But what if the sun were to give too much to man? One must keep in mind that the sun has its great benefits for mankind, but can also possess a very strong and harsh quality towards all of life. With the increasing of pollution by cars and factories from all around the world it has caused our ozone layer to disintegrate more and more each year causing it to grow very thin. Therefore, allowing much more of the sun's ultra violet rays to penetrate deeper into our atmosphere. Thanks to our advancements of our new technology scientists our now able to view the activities which are constantly taking place on the surface of the sun. We are now able to observe and notice that the sun has great tsunami like effects that role throughout its surface. One important fact that should be pointed out to the reader is that of the increasing solar flares that burst out from the sun hundreds of thousands of miles into space with the possibility of disintegrating everything in its path. Fortunately earth is not too close to the sun for it to be wiped out by these powerful solar

"Now as He sat on the Mount of Olives,
the disciples came to Him privately, saying,
'Tell us, when will these things be?'
And 'What will be the sign of Your coming,
and of the end of the Age?'"

Matthew 24:3

"He answered and said to them,
'. . . And there will be famines,'

Matthew 24:7

The great famine which I sense approaching
Will often turn (up in various areas) then become worldwide.
It will be so vast and long-lasting that (people) will grab
Roots from the trees and children from the breast.

Nostradamus
Century I, Quatrain 67

47

The Coming Famine

There has been a plague that has cultivated itself within mankind's existence for many years now. One that has caused man to suffer world wide with great disparity and that has nurtured evil from within his being. That has set a different kind of war aside from all others. That has caused man to destroy himself and cause violent acts to be committed against each other and that have taken the lives of many by the very hands of our brethren. It is the war of food and hunger, greed and gluttony.

It has been said that there is enough food in this world to feed all the people ten times over and that there is no reason why anybody should go through the horrible process of suffering and being hungry. But with all the wars constantly being waged around the globe and the millions of dollars being poured into them who has time to worry about the starving right? I am afraid not. This is another classic case of where funds are going to for the purpose of evil deeds. As mentioned in recent writings why spend billions of dollars on useless wars and battles that cannot be won? Just as the funds should be going to research and development to find cures for sicknesses and other helpful ways to save the lives of many the same should go for the case of food supplies. One thought the reader should be aware of is the fact that we are finding new ways to genetically produce foods of different sorts. And we should be very fortunate for our technology that allows us to produce this, but one must ask, "Are we doing enough?"

It does not take much research to know that the world is coming into a greater food threat and that the scarcity of food is very real. As it has been stated and prophesized by many credible sources the world that we live in is now coming to feel the pain and suffering of famine. There is also the fact that people from all over the world are fighting for food and the fact that small children in many countries will not make it to their teenage years because there is no food to give them strength to survive. Just recent headlines that were released in the year of 2008 showed of people killing each other over a bag of flour. Another headline was that of the farmers in some Asian countries that now have to sleep in their fields just to prevent robberies of their food. It truly is survival of the fittest when it comes down to these types of situations. But one must realize that not only are these poor countries feeling the effect, but the strong ones as well. One can note here that this is another form of evil that thrives within the mind of man.

Genetic Foods

One other very important topic that must be taken into thought is the fact of our increasing technology that we are learning about today that enables us to implement it in various ways such as the use food substances not only for the purpose of feeding animals and people, but to feed machines. When I speak of machines I am speaking in terms of our vehicles which we use for transportation. It is important for one to think that the genetic foods that we are producing will most likely go into these vehicle's tanks rather then the people's stomachs. That is the mind of man.

I am to point out that the food shortages that have been occurring will have the possibility of growing even worse as the years go by unless man is able to do something about it. As the famine becomes wider, so do the battles it will bring amongst the nations and its people.

Man's Micro Enemy

It is the stuff we see in movies and hear of on the news and radio. It is the stuff we hear that can take ones life without warning. All have been affected by it in one way or another. We go to the doctor for it or to our local pharmacy so we can battle against it and get better. It is what can make us stay home from school or work and cause others to stay away *from* us.

For centuries there have been diseases and plagues that have been responsible for the lives of millions of people. From leprosy in the biblical times even to now, to the black plague in the 14th century that was caused by filth and rodents. To malaria that hit many soldiers. Man has had to experience disease and viruses throughout his life here on earth and the many more that are to await him in the future. It should even be noted that the people that possessed diseases many centuries ago were used as a form of a weapon. They would be sent into the camps of the enemy and secretly spread the disease by either means of coughing, sneezing, or in most cases would send the women that had it to seduce the men, therefore destroying the enemy from within. This can also be known as the form we use to today named the biological weapon. Used as a means of containing deadly toxins or can hold a deadly virus, it has been used in the past by certain parties to destroy many. Fortunately now in this day and age thanks to our great sophisticated technology we are able to help cure many of these century old diseases. Or if not cure them, keep them in strict control. What man can be thankful for in regards of our technology is the fact that it is being used for the purpose of good.

Unfortunately there are those viruses that we cannot cure at the time, but to only try and prolong ones life or health. But right now as this is being read there are millions of dollars being poured into research and development to try and discover ways of curing these diseases. I truly believe that more can be poured into research, but again I am to state that there is too much involvement in meaningless and unnecessary battles and wars that are taking billions of dollars away from this kind of research. This is one perfect example why mankind will most likely never learn. As I have stated before and I will always state, it is in mankind's nature to destroy everything.

I am to state a very important note here to the reader and that is one should be extremely aware that there will be new diseases that will come to mankind soon. With all the over the counter medication that is advertised on television and found all over our stores that state one can be healthier by taking or drinking these types of medications that will supposedly fight off bacteria, one can learn that it would most likely bring more harm to the human immune system than good. Now I am to note to the reader that I am speaking of medicine that is used to help make our immune system stronger. The more that a person relies on this type of medicine the more the human body will stop producing its natural immunity and therefore making it worse for the immune system to ward off infections of any type. This can pose as a serious health threat to the people in the event there was to be an outbreak. Many of these medicines have not even been approved by the FDA. With the mysterious strand of mutations that are taking place within common diseases that have been around for many years it will cause new forms that will be able to carry a more powerful potential to do a lot more harm. One can hear in the headlines and read in news articles the possibility of not only pandemics, but epidemics that can dramatically spread all over many regions at an incredible rate taking hundreds of thousand of lives. There is a frightening thought that one must keep in mind and not to be taken too lightly and that is many of today's terrorist and others along with them can get there hands on such forms of viruses and take the initiative to spread them in places that would make a good candidate such as crowded cities and recreational areas. There is the fact that the sophisticated technology we have today can also be used to create new strands of viruses that would be made from the very hands of man. This of course gives us the great example of man's knowledge rapidly growing at an astonishing rate in this modern age. I have spoke of evil within man in the recent writings and this is a perfect example as to what forms evil can be brought to. It must be pointed out that this is another very serious threat which coincides with mankind and that one should think about being prepared *in the event there is to be a full blown outbreak.* **(Now I must strongly point out that one should not become suddenly paranoid and over exaggerate, but to just keep in mind the *possibility* of a threat such as this occurring. Yes, it is very real indeed and another amongst our many warnings and signs that should not be taken too lightly).**

Many medical cures have been extracted from exotic plants and trees for the purpose of good towards mankind. Even to this day one should be aware of the fact that there are still hundreds if not thousands of cures that are yet to be discovered by man hidden amongst the rainforest. The terrible thing is that mankind is destroying what are not only the homes of his fellow brethren, but the many homes and habitats of the wildlife and cures that lay within the plants and trees. And it is all for reasons such as lumber, growing populous, buildings, highways, and much more. Just recently researches are being able to learn new ways of the different types of immune systems that certain types of animals possess that can keep them from catching any bacteria or diseases that can be harmful. Two great examples that I am so eager to share are that of the alligator or crocodiles and the common vulture. I will soon explain what role these two species play in our ever growing research for cures. But first allow me to explain another reason as to what man is doing in terms of destroying. One will notice that when a natural habitat is taken away for certain reasons, those very creatures that once dwelled in them are now forced to travel somewhere else, therefore

53

bringing them into closer contact with humans and in the view of humans, they now pose as a threat. Now since this certain animal is endangering the lives of many it is in human nature to eliminate a threat so that one would not be harmed first. In this case the animal would most likely be killed and from that point on, thus causing it to be classified as an endangered species. Now keep in mind this does not only go for such animals as the crocodile and other large species. It also accounts for the small species that would be deemed a nuisance to the people and their livestock. Now what if these certain animals that were being utterly destroyed possessed a very peculiar nature or natural trait? What if this natural trait that it possessed was a cure that could help millions of untreated people? This is precisely what I am eager to tell of and that is many living creatures of today can help that source of which so blindly expels them from the existence of life. Take for example the alligator- which currently inhabits such areas that have great amounts of bacteria in them which are the swamps. It is the same with the crocodile in other parts of the world. They too live in muddy habitats that are just infested with bacteria. What I am trying to point out here is the fact that our scientists along with the help of wildlife biologists are now questioning on why is it that these creatures can live in filth and not become sick by it. They want to know how strong of an immune system these creatures possess. If the reader can recall the last time they observed a reptile such as a crocodile or alligator whether it be at the zoo or on a show, or even in its natural habitat they would recall the conditions of these habitats. They would also notice all the bacteria that go into their mouths while they eat or just stay submerged in the water. This goes to show that these creatures obviously possess a much greater percentage when it comes to the strength of the immune system than humans.

The same would go with a vulture. Known to be natures clean up crew they scavenge around finding dead carcasses and feed from them. (I must quickly point out the fact that they were given a featherless elongated neck to be able to reach deep inside the dead corps to feed). It does not take one to realize all the bacteria that would have accumulated from the carcass from the moment of death to spread all throughout the body. This is why the scientists of today are studying the immune systems such as this to be able to find a way to better the human species in healthier terms. This is among the great capabilities our technological advancement can help do for the good of mankind.

Another study that is being conducted right now is that of Alzheimer disease. Again thanks to our technology we are now able to draw up three dimensional images of the brains memory core in order to see what the cause is and how we can help prevent it. Here this also plays a part in the environmental destruction that is being done right now. There are millions of plants out there of all types that hold the key medicine used to treat this common disease along with others that are being destroyed. One must be aware that there are people out there that do care and are letting there voices be heard, but since the rest of society and the world are to busy fighting and worrying about who can prevail over the other, it is sad to know that many will go unheard of and the destruction will further continue to grow until all will be a thing of the past.

Environmental Hazards

Millions of pieces of trash are being thrown into our oceans and rivers contaminating them with more and more bacteria each year. As a result from these foolish actions we can find that health and the well being of humanity is at serious risk. another hardship that can be brought upon a whole society or society's is that fact that the more we pollute the more we become involved with our own actions in terms of bringing contaminated substances into our homes such as the air we breathe the water we depend on and other chemical substances as house cleaners and so on. Even the means of transportation that we all depend on today to get us to and from our destinations create a great amount of pollution that is destroying our air we breathe. This is why scientists and engineers are working on different fuel alternatives not only because of the increasing prices, but for the sole purpose of helping to preserve our environment. The same can be observed with other means of energy sources.

"But *as the days of Noah* were,
so *also* will the coming of the Son of Man be . . ."

(Matthew 24:37)

Immoral Corruption From Within

I n these next writings I am to discuss the moral standards of yester years that have deteriorated into immoral practices of this day and age. From the new television shows and movies to the internet and recreational activities for the adult and kids of today to abide by, man is blindly leading themselves into their own destruction through these common practices.

Where Has The Innocence
Of A Child's Mind Gone?

It must be noted to the reader that the child of today is now witnessing and experiencing a lot more activities than a child was to experience around the 1960's and below. Now one can observe a child of today that is being introduced to many of what most would classify as filth and immorality. What is seen today as the "new thing" would have never been heard or thought of in the past years.

In these writings the reader will be introduced to the psychological effect that today's society is bringing to a child and how it will began to mold the child's mind and image without the parents recognition. Here in my recent writings I had mentioned that it all comes down to the child's or children's parents that play the major role in the up bringing of their moral standards. But what about the raising of a child in today's society? What new battles does a parent have to wage against society's opponent? For example, that takes the form of television and music and internet? I am to make a bold statement here *and that is most of the children today will most likely be brought up with no moral standards at all*. As discussed in the *evil within mankind* writings in the previous pages, one can see that a child is most likely going to see wrong and then implement those actions *to* be wrong. The reader can also observe in today's society the way a child addresses an adult, for example, we now hear that the child will most likely over question their parents and talk back much worse today than was thought of years ago. One can also observe the way a child dresses and what music they listen to in order to try and make whatever statement they feel like making. Shows on television are also stating a message to our kids. A great example of the immoral shows that are now coming to television is the new show that promotes sex and glamour towards the kids of today between the ages of twelve to seventeen. Another observation that can be made by one is the fact that kids are now using profanity more and more these days in their everyday conversation. Sadly enough it has become a part of their vocabulary.

A very important note which is to be pointed out to many is that our schools are starting to lose its good moral standards which are suppose to steer the children away from what is immoral. One can hear that a child by the ages of five is now being taught about sexual relationships not only between a man and a woman, but two of the same sex. It also poses as a very serious problem for the child's mind in terms of confusion. A small child of today will now notice two of the same sexes together and married (same sex marriages) other than seeing two of the opposite sexes getting married or living together. This is where the child of today is starting to be molded. Therefore having to be explained, the child is now aware that it is alright in their mind. One can strongly believe that a child of that age should not be taught about these circumstances until a much older age. **There is a very important fact that is to be stated here and that is marriage is solely between a man and woman as it was intended and ever shall be for many future years to come regardless of what many would argue.**

One can find the same with the greater amount of divorces that are taking place these days. We must remember it all comes down to the children which are the ones that observe the types of behaviors that the adults show. Again I am to state that what was once never to be heard of many years ago is now heard of more and more in terms of divorces today. But what do these actions between a married couple pose for a child? We can note that the child is obviously seeing an action of hostility in certain forms whether it be verbal or physical. The child is also told that one of the parents does not like the other and with that bringing the possibility of a child thinking it is their fault, though this specific topic can be further discussed in greater detail, I am to keep with the small examples and basic viewpoints for the reader here.

Another serious concern involving the children of this day and age is the very tool we all turn to for help, whether it is for school, business, or recreation. Yes, this device is called the internet. Not only can a child observe the immorality in today's society on television, but now they can turn to the internet in the privacy of their own room. Now this internet tool can be used for good or for bad. It is now being used for a lot of immorality. Sadly to say with all the immoral corruption that is taking place the children of today are now being introduced to subjects such as these in every day life. We can find that pressure being forced upon the children can also come through peers. But it all boils down to the so called responsible adult and what the children of today are being taught reflex on what moral standards they will bring to the future society of tomorrow. But what are we to make of the ethical standards of many adults in this day and age?

Where Has The Mind Of The Adult Gone?

As children we look up to the adult as a roll model. We were able to observe many actions that were done by our parents and relatives and mimic them. As with animals that are taught at a young age the survival skills for life so are our children of the human species taught on how to act at a young age by the adult.

Today one can observe on television the shows that are broadcasted around the globe and the ones that are soon to come. If you would be able to notice the type of show that is most likely shown and that is the fact that it would promote sex, glamour, violence, (in terms of fighting amongst each over somebody else), and profanity. One must note that the more shows that come on the more of an audience it will bring. Within that audience are the parents that will most likely allow their children to view these programs and therefore mold the child to mimic and think in that way. And later the parent asks the question," Where did I ever go wrong?" It is to be stated that even the adults can be influenced other than children by what they view on television or are around.

"But *know this,*
that *in the last days*
perilous (savage, fierce) times will come,
for men (mankind ... men and women)
will be
lovers of themselves,
lovers of money,
boasters,
proud,
blasphemers,
disobedient to parents,
unthankful,
unholy, unloving, unforgiving,
slanderers,
without self-control,
violent (brutal),
despisers of good,
traitors,
headstrong,
arrogant (haughty),
lovers of pleasure
rather than lovers of God,
having a *form* of godliness but denying its power ..."

Timothy 3:1-5

It must be noted that this *is* the society of today. That this society wants nothing more than sex, violence, greed, fame, pride, to see someone else be hurt other then them, to laugh and mock the good and moral and the righteousness, to deceive and to lie... what has our society become?

All Is Quiet

Now we have come to the realization on what can cause the destruction of the human species, therefore bringing us to the conclusion as to why man's fate is possibly close at hand. All that has been read in the recent pages will each hold and play their key role on this earth and with mankind that will determine the outcome of his destiny.

In the beginning pages of these writings the reader may recall that there are to be a few credible sources that one can look to in regards of man and his fate. There is that of the bible codes and Nostradamus, and that of the Mayan Calendar and its mysterious predictions, along with the planetary alignment that will soon take its place and the most credible one of all, the book of revelations from the bible. What the reader must be aware of is the fact that there is an eerie feeling that plagues the air when trying to figure out if something will take place in the event of a major catastrophe. I truly believe right now things will remain quite perhaps for the next year (2008-2009). But what one must realize is that while things seem quiet right now they are slowly stirring around the world becoming ready to explode unleashing its great wrath. We must look at one very important fact. And that is the dates that are given by all these credible sources. If one was to realize that these dates were to some how mysteriously fall into place side by side and that they come to being a year away from each other, one could not help but notice the sense it would bring to a very high probability the harm mankind would soon feel. For example: the Mayan calendar ends on December 21, **2012**, but does this mean the world is going to end? I would say that the probability of it ending on this date would most likely not be. I believe that it may be the beginning of a new cycle and the end of an old. What the Mayan people are trying to say is that it most likely may mean the start of a new era for man or may also be put, the beginning of a new dawn. I believe that a major catastrophic event may occur at or around this year. Now we will draw from the source of the bible codes. In one of the codes it is predicted and found in the matrix that there will be a great asteroid that will involve earth and mankind. When was the date set for this event? It is set for the year **2010**. Another somewhat credible source that we are relying on is that of Nostradamus which was mentioned in the recent writings. And what is to happen in 2011? It should be stated that out of all the dates there is why do they all fall at or around the same years? Out of all these years that these bible codes were hidden, why were they suddenly discovered in these perilous times we live in? It is not just coincident, but for a reason. There is to be a very important note for the reader and that is the fact that all still remains quiet for now, but between the year 2010 and up to 2012 one should be extremely aware that there is going to a *very high possibility* of major disasters and catastrophic events that will unfold simultaneously which will have an enormous impact on that of mankind.

Another very interesting subject that should be pointed out to the reader is the fact that if we again observe the Doomsday Clock attentively one can notice that five minutes away from twelve midnight can count as five years away from a major catastrophic global event whether it be made natural or by man. Now if we take that five minutes and turn it into five years and add to that the year the dial was just recently moved which was on January 17th 2007 we can note that it will add up to twelve or 2012. Or we can put it as 2007 + 5 years = **2012**. So we can now observe that this Doomsday Clock is among one of the credible sources that also falls at or around those years among 2012. The year that is said to have a major event brought upon mankind. Does this all sound like a Coincident? As was stated before, ***everything happens for a reason.* And I believe that this is all happening for a great and important reason...**

65

Yes, things may seem relatively calm and quiet for now, but most likely soon in a few years that pot will boil over and burn man's fate. We must all go on living our normal lives, but with the thought that we should be prepared for what might come as we normally would prepare ourselves for disasters. We must ask ourselves, what is really going to happen when the planets do align with each other? Is the shifting of the polarities really going to have a major effect on the seasons and weather? And can it actually cause severe catastrophic disasters all around the world and devastate mankind? Do the modern nations of today possess the quality of Ancient Rome? And bring itself to a downfall as with Rome did? With the ever increasing rate of violence escalating in the society of today brings forth new fears of the individual's safety.

There is good in this world, but if man continues to take the path which he so blindly treads he will always cause the evil to outweigh the good.

What it was many years ago can be no more today and the years to come. From the days of Noah and his ark to that of the destruction of Sodom and Gomorra evil has been washed away and will again be washed away once more.

There is one thing that the reader should be fully aware of. And that is no man can ever foresee the exact date and time when the world is going to come to its end. But we can only be prepared for when it does...

Man treads in the very darkness of his consummation in this world that was graciously handed to him. Should he choose to bring about the final destruction of it, so let it be written and sealed with the mark of failure...

Remember: things do not change...people change...

"The Earth was *corrupt* (like smelly, rotting meat ... *immoral*)
before God,
and the Earth was *filled with violence*.
So God looked upon the Earth,
and indeed it was corrupt;
for all flesh had corrupted their way on the Earth.
And God said to Noah,
'The end of all flesh has come before Me,
for the Earth is filled with violence through them;
and behold, I will destroy them with the Earth . . .'"

Genesis 6:11-13

The great day of their wrath has come and who is able to stand.

Revelations 6: 17

CPSIA information can be obtained at www.ICGtesting.com
Printed in the USA
BVOW080410020413

317007BV00003B/430/P